QUESTIONS TO ASK
BEFORE LEAVING

To Your Answers

BY ERIN BROWN JOURNALED
BY EMILY NITCHER

ISBN: 1726234193

ISBN-13: 978-1726234191

DEDICATION

To Kimbra. Thank you for listening to every thought that is ever in my head. For getting me through. And for always leading me back to myself.

INTRODUCTION

I have left many things. Some people call it quitting. I wonder about the implication that leaving is a failure. Or maybe it is believing you have given your all and are now making a new choice. Is it pious to stay where you don't belong? Or stick to a place that doesn't bring you joy? Whether approaching a career change, a location change, or any other major change… I have found the best advice always sends me back to my heart. But advice rarely suffices, much of anything really. We have to find ourselves in our lives. Understand the person in the mirror. What we long for and what we know and where we stand. We are the only ones able to wonder about what is possible for us and pursue it. Sometimes in a leap of faith. Sometimes with every piece of evidence on our side. Sometimes without a net. Every time I have left anything, I was unable to answer some of these questions well. It's imperfect. No system of understanding ourselves makes sense to me, save personal inquiry. I hope these questions foster and inquiry with yourself that allows you to feel free in your life. Whatever that means to and for you.

DO YOU PLAN ESCAPE ROUTES IN YOUR HEAD?

THINK ABOUT

HOW THINGS

→ COULD BE ←

DIFFERENT?

WONDER ABOUT THE WAY OUT?

ARE YOU SCARED?

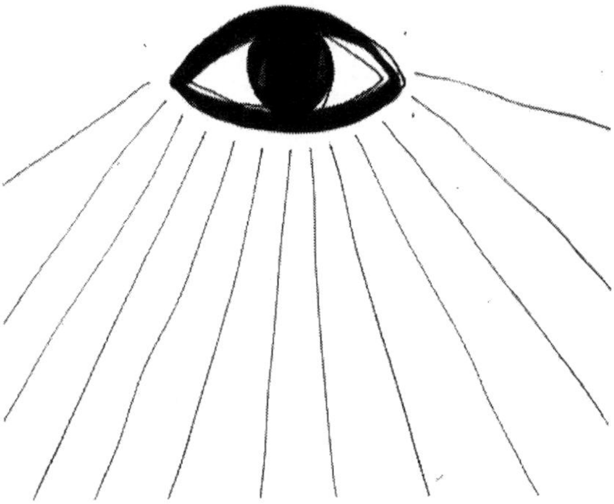

WHAT ARE YOU
SCARED OF, LOVE?
IS THE COMFORT
OF FAMILIAR THE
DRAW?
IS THIS THE BEST
FAMILIAR YOU COULD
KNOW?

HOW COULD YOU SHOW UP? DIFFERENTLY?

HAVE YOU

TRIED

THIS?

DOES IT FEEL LIKE

YOU?

LIKE HOME?

ARE YOU

ASKING

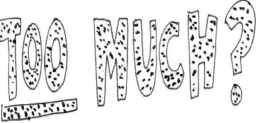

TOO MUCH?

WHAT DOES THAT
MEAN?

WOULD YOU BELIEVE
SOMEONE ELSE
ASKING FOR THE
SAME THINGS WAS
ASKING FOR TOO
MUCH?

WHAT DO YOU
BELIEVE YOU
DESERVE?

9

WHEN DID IT
START?

DID YOU LEARN IT
SOMEWHERE?

IS THAT A LIFE
YOU WANT?

DOES IT HURT?

WHEN?

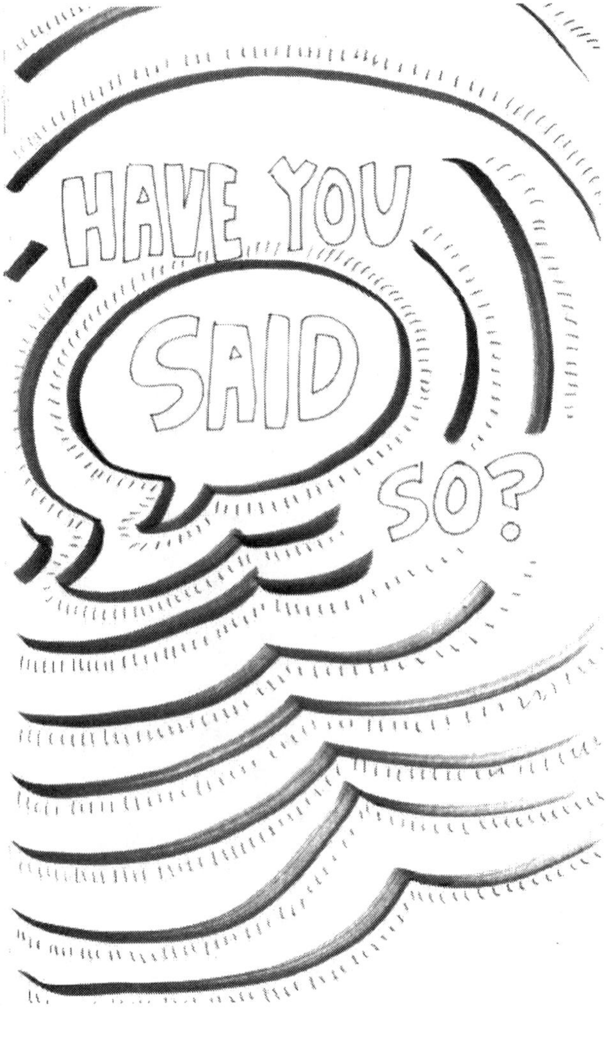
HAVE YOU
SAID
SO?

WERE YOU HEARD?

DID YOU FEEL SAFE TO SAY SO?

DO YOU KNOW *WHERE* THE PAIN LIVES?

HAVE YOU FELT IT
BEFORE?

DOES IT HAVE
A NAME?

IS THIS A PAIN
YOU KEEP CHOOSING?

DOES IT MOVE?

CHANGE COLOR?

LESSEN?

IS IT HERE?

HAVE YOU ALWAYS
WANTED IT?

HAVE YOU RECENTLY
ALLOWED YOURSELF
TO WANT SOMETHING
ELSE?

WHY?

HOW COULD IT BE DIFFERENT?

IS THAT
POSSIBLE?

IS IT REAL?

IS IT A
STORY?

WHAT DOES IT
MEAN TO LOSE?

HAVE YOU ALREADY
LOST IT?

WHAT ARE YOU
HOLDING ONTO?

CAN YOU FEEL IT?

IS IT A STORY?

IS IT WORTH
CHASING?

IS IT BEAUTIFUL?

IS IT WORTH IT, WHATEVER THE CHOICE ?

WHAT DOES
THAT MEAN?

WHAT RISKS ARE
YOU READY TO
TAKE?

ARE YOU LIVING A PATTERN?

IS IT HEALTHY?

DID YOU LEARN
IT SOMEWHERE?

HOW DOES IT
FEEL?

ARE YOU HEALTHY?

IS THAT A
GOOD PLACE
TO START?

WHERE IS YOUR VOICE?

IS IT FREE HERE?

DOES IT FEEL
SAFE?

VALUED?

ARE YOU
LISTENING?

Was there a pang when you read that?

ARE YOU TIRED?

WHAT DOES THAT MEAN?

IF IT IS, SHOULD YOU STAY?

WHAT DOES THAT MEAN?

DID SOMETHING BREAK?

CAN IT BE REPAIRED?

ARE YOU BEING HONEST?

WITH WHO?

YOURSELF?

DO YOU

FEEL

RESPECTED?

LOVED?

CHERISHED?

VALUED?

APPRECIATED?

SUPPORTED?

ARE YOU
GIVING THOSE
THINGS?

ARE THEY RECEIVED WITH LOVE?

DO YOU BELIEVE
YOU DESERVE
THOSE THINGS?

(IF NOT, WHY LOVE?)

...MAYBE START
THERE.

IS THIS WHAT

YOU WANTED?

HAS THAT

CHANGED?

WHAT DO YOU
KNOW NOW
THAT YOU
DIDN'T KNOW
THEN?

ABOUT YOURSELF?

DID YOU GIVE IT YOUR BEST?

(DOES YOUR BEST

MEAN SACRIFICE?

HOW MUCH?

DOES IT TAKE

MORE THAN

IT GIVES?))

HOW DO YOU KNOW WHEN YOU'RE DONE?

HAVE YOU
BEEN DONE
BEFORE?

WHAT DID IT FEEL
LIKE?

ARE YOU YOUR BEST HERE?

YOU ARE HERE

IS YOUR BEST
RECEIVED HERE?

HOW IS YOUR HEART?

IS YOUR BEST
RECEIVED HERE?

HOW IS YOUR HEART?

WHEN IS IT MOST ALIVE?

HOW IS YOUR HEART?

WHEN IS IT MOST NUMB?

WHY?

IN WHAT WAY?

IS IT LIMITED?

WHY?

DO YOU LAUGH?
DO YOU DANCE?
ARE YOU JOYFUL?
DO YOU PLAY?

ARE YOU
SUPPORTED
IN WAYS
YOU CAN
FEEL?

HOW DO YOU
FEEL SUPPORTED?

IS IT AN ACTION?

A FEELING?

ARE YOU

APPRECIATIVE

? ? ? ? ? ? ? ? ? ? ?

(OF WHAT? HOW?)

DO YOU FEEL AT HOME?

➡ WHAT IS A
HOME?

SECURITY?

SAFETY?

PEACE?

FAMILIARITY?

LOVE?

JOY?

CAN YOU FLY?

IS IT HERE?

ABOUT THE CREATORS

Erin Brown is a writer, activist and co-founder of Ferine Mag. This is her forth book and the first in a series of journals to help process emotions. She hails from and currently resides in Lawrence, Kansas. When she's not taking on the world by making things, you can find her slinging burgers at Ladybird Diner. Happiest on a dance floor.

Emily Nitcher is an avid journaler since the fourth grade, Emily was born and raised in Lawrence, KS. She double majored in art history and painting at Drake University in Des Moines, IA, and currently resides in Prairie Village, KS with her dog Roy. When she's not journaling, she can be found consulting her tarot decks and star charts, communicating with Spirit, or outside, preferably with friends and animals.